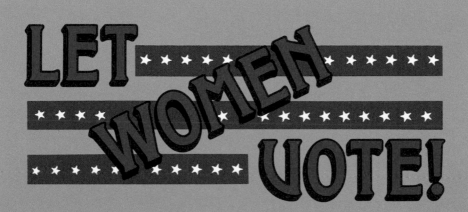

LET WOMEN VOTE!

BY MARLENE TARG BRILL

Spotlight on American History
The Millbrook Press • Brookfield, Connecticut

Library of Congress Cataloging-in-Publication Data
Brill, Marlene Targ.
Let women vote! / by Marlene Targ Brill.
p.   cm. — (Spotlight on American history)
Includes bibliographical references and index.
Summary: Discusses the fight for the passage of the Nineteenth
Amendment, which granted all women the right to vote when it was
ratified in 1920.
ISBN 1-56294-589-0 (lib. bdg.)
1. Women—Suffrage—United States—History—Juvenile literature.
[1. Women—Suffrage. 2. Women's rights.] I. Title. II. Series.
JK1898.B75 1996 324.6'23'0973—dc20 95-22783 CIP AC

Cover photograph courtesy of Bettmann Archive
Photographs courtesy of Sophia Smith Collection, Smith College: pp. 6, 9, 18,
36; UPI/Bettmann: pp. 11, 47, 56; Library of Congress: p. 12; Culver Pictures: pp.
16, 22 (top); North Wind Picture Archives: pp. 17, 45; Bettmann: p. 22 (bottom)
27 (bottom), 32, 51; Seneca Falls Historical Society: pp. 27 (top), 34; Women's
Rights National Historical Park, National Park Service: p. 28; Museum of the City
of New York: p. 40, (Ben Shahn, *Women's Christian Temperance Union Parade*).

Published by The Millbrook Press, Inc.
2 Old New Milford Road, Brookfield, Connecticut 06804

Contents

Let Women Vote!

*Carrie Chapman Catt as she appeared in a parade
celebrating the passage of the Nineteenth Amendment,
which gave women the right to vote.*

1

****

FIGHT TO THE FINISH

In July 1920, Carrie Chapman Catt received an urgent telegram: Come to Nashville, Tennessee, it read, and come quickly! The state had turned into a bitter battlefield. Tennessee women needed Catt, the national leader of the suffragist movement, to lead the final fight in the struggle for woman suffrage, the right to vote.

Governor Albert H. Roberts had called a special session of Tennessee lawmakers, or legislators. They were to vote on a change in the United States Constitution. The new Nineteenth Amendment required approval by thirty-six states before becoming law. Tennessee's vote was critical. Thirty-five states had already approved the amendment, which said:

> *The right of citizens of the United States to vote shall not be denied or abridged [limited] by the United States or by any state on account of sex.*

In simpler words, the amendment granted women the right to vote.

Catt packed a small overnight bag at once. She expected to stay in Nashville only a few days, long enough to prove that the women worried needlessly. After she arrived, however, Catt changed her mind. Men and women who opposed the vote had flooded into Nashville. The size and strength of groups against woman suffrage shocked her. Catt quickly sent home for more clothes. For the next six weeks she fought one of the toughest battles in the seventy-two-year-long suffrage war.

Catt's first job was to put an end to the conflicts that divided the many women's groups within the state. She wrote a series of letters to their leaders. The sixty-two-year-old woman appealed to their love of country. She challenged suffrage workers to oppose anyone who dared deny voting rights to half the citizens. Catt's powerful words sparked unity. The Tennessee women buried their differences. They accepted Catt's plan and promised to approach lawmakers as one voice.

Next, Catt went on a speaking tour of large Tennessee cities. She held meetings with local suffrage leaders and called for a poll of Tennessee legislators. Which way would they vote? Was anyone undecided? The women asked each man to sign a pledge to vote for suffrage.

Another reason for the tour was to let Tennessee women know what was happening in Nashville. The fight was for more than the state. It was for an entire nation to resist bullies in the liquor, railroad, and manufacturing trades. These companies feared that women were against the sale of alcohol and for the improvement of factory working conditions. A woman's vote would be bad for business!

Antisuffrage workers tried every trick to sway state representatives and senators to their side. They spread rumors about the governor, who was up for reelection in November. They threatened lawmakers with ruin of their businesses or political careers. Antisuffrage men offered some lawmakers rewards while accusing others of accepting money for votes. One legislator received kidnapping threats. Catt returned to Nashville discouraged.

As the special session neared, antis (anti-suffragists) from across the country swarmed into Nashville. They attacked the public and private lives of suffrage workers. "Mrs. Catt Defames Her Country" shouted one handbill. Antis stole suffragist telegrams and spied outside windows and doors. Catt received many unsigned letters filled with nasty insults.

Antisuffrage cartoons perpetuated the myth that women neglected their homes and families for the suffragist cause.

The night before the first session Catt noticed lawmakers disappear into a room on the hotel's eighth floor, where antis were offering them free drinks. Catt wrote later in *Women Suffrage and Politics:*

As the evening grew late, legislators, both suffrage and anti-suffrage men, were reeling through the halls. . . . Hour by hour suffrage men and women who went to the different hotels of the city to talk with the legislators, came back to the Hermitage headquarters to report. And every report told the same story—the Legislature was drunk!

Lawmakers finally met on a hot, muggy August 9. Four days later the Tennessee Senate approved the Nineteenth Amendment by a vote of twenty-five to four. Then the fight heated up in the House. In an unexpected move, House Speaker Seth Walker spoke against suffrage. And he had signed a pledge!

For another week both sides tried to delay the vote, hoping other House members would change their mind. Suffrage men and women guarded their members. They took lawmakers to movies, for rides in the country, anywhere away from the enemy. Picketers patrolled the railway station night and day to keep legislators and their votes in town.

On August 18, those against suffrage called for a vote, sure they would win. The count was closer than expected, however. Ninety-six representatives voted, out of ninety-nine. One man arrived from his hospital bed to vote for suffrage. Another jumped from a moving train. He was going home to see his dying wife when suffrage supporters promised him a special train if he stayed.

Two painfully slow roll calls ended in a tie. The amendment still needed two more votes to pass. The speaker announced another roll call. This time twenty-four-year-old Harry Burn followed his mother's advice. "Hurrah! And vote for suffrage and don't keep them in doubt," Mrs. Burn had written in a letter to her son.

Harry Burn voted *yes*. Passage required one more vote. Banks Turner, the governor's friend, switched sides and cast the final *yes*. The suffrage amendment passed by a vote of forty-nine to forty-seven.

Suffragettes hold a celebration following their victory in 1920.

Constitutional Amendments

ALL UNITED STATES CITIZENS must follow the same basic laws. Many of these laws were created when the country began. Our nation's founders wrote them into a paper called the Constitution for future generations to follow.

The Constitution tells how lawmakers, or legislators, are chosen by the people and how they should run the nation's government through Congress. Legislators make up two houses in Congress: the House of Representatives and the Senate. The House includes one representative for every 30,000 people in a state. The Senate contains two senators from each state, no matter how many people live in that state.

Since its creation in 1776, the Constitution has remained mostly unchanged. Yet twenty-six times, Congress decided to change, or amend, the Constitution. The nineteenth change was the amendment that gave women the right to vote.

Three fourths of the members in each house of Congress must pass an amendment. Then three fourths of the state legislatures must approve an amendment before it becomes part of the Constitution.

The joy of victory was short. House rules permitted another vote within three days. Antisuffrage men seized the chance for more dirty tricks. They charged Harry Burn with taking bribes. Burn successfully disproved the charges. Then antis sent a woman to urge Burn's mother to deny her letter. Mrs. Burn was furious. She quickly wrote her son again. "I stand squarely behind suffrage and request my son to stick to suffrage until the end." Burn held to his vote.

Tennessee governor Roberts approved the amendment and sent a copy to Washington, DC. On August 26, Secretary of State Bainbridge Colby signed the Woman Suffrage Amendment into the United States Constitution.

Catt addressed new voters in the September 4, 1920, issue of *The Woman Citizen:*

The vote is the . . . guarantee of your liberty. Women have suffered agony of soul which you never can comprehend, that you and your daughters might inherit political freedom. That vote has been costly. Prize it!

2

★ ★

AN UPHILL BATTLE

Women played an important role in building the United States. As pioneers, they ran the household and helped to clear land and build towns. A few colonies let women own property, and sometimes widows who owned property were allowed to vote on minor affairs. But as the United States expanded, fixed ideas about what was proper for women spread throughout the country. Few women before the mid-1800s dared think seriously about voting.

From the beginning, voting rights usually belonged to white men only. These men owned land and made the laws. That's the way it had always been in England. And settlers continued that custom in the new land.

In 1776, the year the colonies declared their independence, New Jersey's constitution gave the vote to men and women "of full age who are worth fifty pounds [English dollars]." No one expected women to vote. And in fact, only 2 of 258 women took advantage of their right in the next Burlington, New Jersey, election.

By 1797, however, women were voting in larger numbers. Outraged lawmakers worried that women could vote them out of office. Many complained that government would soon overflow "with petticoats."

For the next ten years, New Jersey lawmakers argued about restricting women's right to vote. Finally, the 1807 legislature fell in line with other new states. New Jersey limited the vote to white men who owned property.

Without question, a woman's place was in the home. And even there, women had many duties but few rights. Women made soap and cleaned, washed laundry, churned butter, and prepared meals. They milked cows, made candles, spun thread and yarn, sewed clothes, and raised the children. Any woman who complained was quickly quieted. She was only one very tired voice.

THE IDEA that women belonged at home came in part from English common law. Under common law, women who married surrendered all rights to their husband. "Man and wife are one person," a 1632 document read. "To be a married woman, her new self is . . . her master."

Most early American women could not own property or sign contracts. Their husbands owned their clothes, household goods, and anything they brought to the marriage. If a woman earned wages, they belonged to her husband. Before 1840, Massachusetts law prohibited women from spending money, even money collected from a women's sewing club, unless a man approved.

When a husband died, his wife could lose everything unless the man wrote a will that detailed what she should receive. Even with the will, a wife only gained part of her dead husband's property. Most states limited a woman to one third of her husband's holdings.

A father's word was law for children, too. A man could send his children to learn a trade or be raised by someone else without their mother's consent. Divorce between husband and wife was almost impossible. And if a divorce was granted, the woman lost all rights to her children, no matter how badly the father behaved.

After visiting the United States, French author Alexis de Tocqueville wrote, "No people, with the exception of slaves, had less rights over themselves in eighteenth-century and early nineteenth-century America than married women."

In this sketch of a kitchen in 1876, women are shown in their "rightful place."

Wife auctions, more common in England than America,
demonstrated the notion of women as property.

Religion further bound a woman to her husband. "Thy desire shall be to thy husband, and he shall rule over thee," said the Bible. Most colonial religious groups, except the Quakers, taught that women were less than men. Men could speak for God. A woman's role was to marry and produce children.

Laws and the church defined a woman's place. But lack of higher education kept her there. Fathers saw no need for daughters to receive more than a basic education. With few exceptions, girls were raised to be good daughters, sisters, wives, and mothers.

"I am acquainted with a sensible girl who is anxious to improve her mind, but her father . . . endeavours [tries] to convince her that all knowledge, except that of domestic [household] affairs, appears unbecoming in a female," wrote a woman named Sarah Bradford in an 1809 letter to a friend.

Lucy Stone, an early suffrage worker, had to fight for the right to further her education.

Lucy Stone, a famous suffrage worker, gathered nuts and berries as a young child. She sold them to pay for schoolbooks her father refused to buy for her. When she reached her early teens, he ordered Lucy to leave school. After much pleading, her father agreed to lend her money for college, even though he gladly paid for her brothers' education.

Lucy went to Oberlin College in Ohio. Oberlin was the only college in the country open to women and blacks during the 1830s. Even there, Lucy fought for the right to debate, speak in public, and read her graduation essay. She lost each battle, but she did become the first Massachusetts woman to earn a college degree.

[18]

Women who fought for more education faced many difficulties. The most common was the popular notion that women had smaller brains than men. Most people believed higher mathematics or science or money matters taxed a woman's limited mind. In a 1790 essay about women, Judith Murray asked:

> *Will it be said the judgment of a male two years old is more sage [wise] than that of a female's of the same age? I believe the reverse is . . . true. . . . The one [boy] is taught to aspire, the other [girl] is early confined and limited.*

Indeed, daughters of the wealthy had time and money for education. Yet they merely learned to sing, paint, and improve their needlework.

By the 1800s, isolated women's voices began to cry out for fairer treatment. They challenged their husbands, fathers, and brothers. They questioned the church, lawmakers, and teachers. Still, what they needed was a way to meet other women and men who held the same views.

3

★ ★

THE RIGHTS OF WOMEN AND SLAVES

The growing protest against slavery gave women a reason to come together. Many men and women disapproved of one person owning another. The practice of importing slaves from Africa had been outlawed since 1808. Yet American lawmakers refused to force owners to free their slaves. Churches began to encourage women to move beyond the home to help end slavery.

Members of religious groups, many of them Quakers, led the movement to end, or abolish, slavery. They formed a secret route to freedom in the northern United States and Canada, called the Underground Railroad. Men needed women to help feed, clothe, and sometimes lead runaway slaves to the next safe house along the route. With these brave acts, women earned a place in the antislavery (abolitionist) movement.

In the 1820s and 1830s, the voices against slavery grew stronger. Many brave women came forward. Maria Stewart was one of the first black women to speak in public. For two years she urged audiences to end slavery. She also pressed for schools to teach black girls who were barred from formal education. But a woman speaking in public was still unthinkable in the 1830s. Stinging insults finally forced Stewart from public life.

Lucretia Mott was not so easily silenced. She was a Quaker who had been raised as a man's equal. Yet, as a teacher, she had known the injustice of earning less pay than a man for the same job.

At age twenty-eight, Mott became a minister and a champion of the abolitionist cause. Soon her quiet but commanding speeches against slavery brought her fame. Lucretia and her husband, James, secretly offered their home as a station along the Underground Railroad.

In 1833, James Mott helped found the American Anti-Slavery Society in Philadelphia. The society permitted women to attend meetings but refused them membership. Lucretia Mott objected. Within a few weeks, she had organized women into the first Female Anti-Slavery Society.

Similar societies developed in most major cities in the Northeast. Freed black women created their own organizations in the North and West. Members of these societies held meetings, sold antislavery pamphlets, and gathered names on petitions to send to Congress.

Petitions called for new states to be free of slavery. They protested against the sale of slaves across state lines. In 1834, Southerners, many of whom defended slavery, introduced a bill that outlawed petitions to the House of Representatives.

Speaking against slavery was dangerous. Angry mobs stormed meeting halls. They sometimes burned buildings where antislavery gatherings were held. Crowds pelted homes and offices of society leaders with rocks, eggs, or bricks.

*One of the best-known social reformers,
Lucretia Mott took up the cause against slavery
and for women's suffrage.*

Antislavery meetings often turned into debates over women's suffrage issues.

Women drew the worst attacks. They offended listeners because of their ideas *and* because speaking in public was seen as unwomanly.

After abolitionists Angelina and Sarah Grimké toured New England, Massachusetts clergy issued a strong letter attacking their speeches. Churches throughout the state read the letters condemning the women. The clergy claimed that "when a woman assumes the place and tone of man as public reformer . . . her character becomes unnatural."

Sarah Grimké answered the clergy in a series of letters. She argued that they misquoted the Bible to keep women down. She wanted equal rights for women.

"All I ask our brethren is, that they will take their feet from off our necks and permit us to stand upright on that ground which God designed us to occupy," she wrote. Angelina Grimké further urged women not to obey limits commonly set on what they could achieve.

William Lloyd Garrison published the letters in *The Liberator*, his weekly antislavery newspaper. From then on, women's rights were linked to the fight against slavery. Women dared to wonder aloud whether they had any more rights than a slave.

Antislavery women broke new ground. They wrote articles on behalf of women. They spoke in public. They learned to organize groups and gather names for petitions. They heard voices of other women and men who championed their equality. These voices formed a network of women prepared to embrace fresh ideas. What they needed now were leaders and a plan.

4

★ ★

BIRTH OF WOMEN'S RIGHTS

In the summer of 1840, Lucretia Mott and Elizabeth Cady Stanton traveled to the World Anti-Slavery Convention in London. William Lloyd Garrison had chosen Lucretia Mott to represent the Philadelphia Anti-Slavery Society. By then, the gentle woman in white cap and gray Quaker dress was forty-seven years old and the mother of five children.

Stanton came to London with her new husband, Henry. He was sent by the American Anti-Slavery Society. The daughter of a wealthy New York judge, Elizabeth Stanton had learned many bitter lessons as a girl. When Stanton earned top honors in Greek class, Judge Cady said, "Ah, you should have been a boy!"

Young Elizabeth often hid in her father's law office. She overheard women reveal painful stories about husbands who beat them, stole their money, or sold their land. Each time Judge Cady said he could do nothing under the law. Elizabeth vowed to change the laws so that women would be treated more fairly.

Because she was a girl, Elizabeth would have no chance of going to law school. This did not stop her from studying her father's law books. As an adult Elizabeth Stanton protested in other small ways. When she married, she insisted that the word "obey" be cut from the wedding vows. To "love and honor" her husband was quite enough.

The London conference proved disappointing to Mott and Stanton. The two women arrived to find that their seats were in the gallery behind a curtain. Conference leaders refused to allow women delegates to take part. Mott protested, and the men voted again. But the ban remained. Stanton and Mott left to tour London rather than stay and say nothing.

Elizabeth Cady Stanton was twenty-two years younger than Lucretia Mott. Yet the two women formed an instant bond. Both questioned why women should work for a cause, such as ending slavery, without equal say. They wanted the legal right to do whatever a man could do. The women agreed to take action when they returned to America. But they were unclear as to the form this action should take.

Once home, Mott resumed preaching, speaking against slavery, and tending her family. Elizabeth and Henry Stanton moved to Boston and then to Seneca Falls, New York. There, Elizabeth strained under the daily grind of housework and raising three lively boys.

Over the next eight years, the two women wrote letters. Mott shared her beliefs about women as free thinkers. She suggested books to feed Stanton's hungry mind. Stanton wrote of her growing unhappiness. Henry traveled often. Elizabeth felt like the sad and trapped women who came to her father's office.

*I*N JULY 1848, Mott wrote Stanton that she planned to visit her sister, Martha Wright, near Seneca Falls. Jane Hunt of nearby Waterloo invited Stanton, Mott, Wright, and Mary Ann McClintock to tea. At the July 13 tea, Stanton admitted to the women how truly miserable she was.

> *I poured out, that day, the torrent of my . . . long discontent, with such vehemence and indignation [bitterness] that I stirred myself, as well as the rest of the party, to do and dare anything.*

The five women agreed that the time was right to break the silence. They would call a meeting to discuss the causes of women's problems.

The following day, Stanton announced the Woman's Rights Convention in the *Seneca County Courier*. The notice read:

> *A convention to discuss the social, civil, and religious rights of woman will be held in the Wesleyan Chapel, Seneca Falls, New York, on Wednesday and Thursday, the 19th and 20th of July.*

The next morning the women met to plan the meeting and prepare a statement of basic women's rights. At first, Stanton searched through papers from antislavery meetings for ideas. Then she read the United States Declaration of Independence. How fitting to pattern their call for rights after the country's call for freedom!

Stanton rewrote the Declaration to include the word *women:* "We hold these truths to be self-evident: that all men and women are created equal. . . ." Then the women agreed on a list of demands for true equality with men. They included the right to earn wages, go to college, own property, pursue a career, have equal say about children after divorce, and be heard in court.

REPORT

OF THE

WOMAN'S RIGHTS

CONVENTION,

Held at SENECA FALLS, N. Y., July 19th
and 20th, 1848.

Jane Camus

ROCHESTER:
PRINTED BY JOHN DICK
AT THE NORTH STAR OFFICE.

The Report of the Woman's Rights Convention, a two-day meeting held in 1848 to discuss the "Social, Civil, and Religious Condition of Woman."

A cartoon showing the reaction of spectators to a speaker at the Woman's Rights Convention. Of all the demands the speakers made, the demand for the right to vote sparked the most heated debate.

A plaque commemorating the 1848 Woman's Rights Convention and its organizer, Elizabeth Cady Stanton, at the Women's Rights National Historical Park in Seneca Falls, New York.

Stanton added one more demand—the right to vote. Voting had allowed men to pass laws that robbed women of control over their lives. Stanton claimed the only way to secure the other rights was for women to change the laws themselves.

Some women feared that wanting the vote went too far. Lucretia Mott argued, "Thou will make us ridiculous. We must go slowly." Later, Elizabeth read the proposal to Henry Stanton. Usually he agreed with women's rights. This time, however, he left town rather than be connected with his wife's crazy idea.

On July 19, 1848, more than three hundred people traveled by foot or horsedrawn wagon to the Seneca Falls chapel. The first meeting day was for women only. But the women had little training with running meetings. They decided James Mott should lead the group, which included about forty men.

The second day Elizabeth Stanton gave her first public speech. Her brilliant words rang through the church:

We are assembled . . . to declare our right to be free as man is free, . . . to have such disgraceful laws as give man the power to . . . imprison his wife . . . erased from our statute books.

Then she read the list of demands. The right to vote sent shock waves through the meeting. After heated debate, the convention ended. Before leaving, sixty-eight women and thirty-two men signed the Declaration of Sentiments. Everyone agreed on all but one point. Still, the demand for the right to vote passed. With its passage came a new feeling.

Seneca Falls showed women they were not alone in their discontent. Now women could hope for a life beyond that of wife and mother. They dared to dream of a time when their rights would equal a man's—including the right to vote.

5

★ ★

CIVIL WAR YEARS

The 1848 convention brought a storm of protest. Newspapers belittled the women for their bold declarations. The *Mechanics Advocate* of Albany, New York, claimed that "the order of things established at the creation of mankind, and continued six thousand years, would be completely broken up."

The Reverend Henry Bellows warned about the downfall of a woman who spoke "unbonneted and unshawled before the public gaze." Men worried that a woman's freedom would leave her unprotected. Stanton argued that women would rather protect themselves with the right to vote.

News about the Seneca Falls meeting spread. Women across the country prepared their own meetings. This time, they ran programs without men. Stanton wrote of her next meeting, two years later in Salem, Ohio: "For the first time in the world's history men learned how it felt to sit in silence when questions in which they were interested were under discussion."

The first National Women's Rights Convention followed in Worcester, Massachusetts, in 1850. This meeting drew more than one thousand people from eleven states. The convention resulted in an eight-state petition drive for women's right to vote. Volunteers were to sign one hundred and fifty backers from each state.

These petitions signaled the first attempts to gain the vote for women by influencing legislators. Neither the petitions nor women's rights attracted much interest, though. Still, national women's conventions met every year except 1857 for the next ten years.

Many changes swept through the country during the 1850s and 1860s. All white men over the age of twenty-one gained the right to vote. When gold fever struck in California, more pioneers headed west. Industry expanded throughout the East and Midwest. Telegraph lines and railroad tracks stretched across the nation. These links between regions and communities spread the Seneca Falls ideas about women.

Several states granted married women the right to own property. It became acceptable for poor women to earn wages outside the home. By 1850 one million people worked in factories. Of these, one quarter were women.

In the East, many women moved from farms to factory towns. City girls traveled west looking for gold, husbands, or freedom. Only the South stayed much the same. Slavery kept black and white women isolated on large plantations.

*T*HE NEW suffrage movement attracted strong women who worked for social change. After graduating from Oberlin College in 1847, Lucy Stone had become a speaker for the Massachusetts Anti-Slavery Society. Her clear, bell-like voice calmed the angriest crowds. Stone attended the Worcester convention. From then on, her speeches stressed rights for women and blacks.

Susan Brownell Anthony followed news about the Seneca women closely. At first, her interests were in other causes. Anthony questioned the fact she earned less than a man as a teacher. When her protests went unanswered, Anthony quit teaching. She then turned to the temperance movement, which pushed for outlawing the sale of alcohol. Anthony saw how unfair laws forced women to stay married to alcoholic husbands. She soon learned men in temperance groups also treated women unfairly.

At one Rochester temperance meeting "sisters were not invited to speak," remembered Anthony, "but to listen and learn." She stormed out, followed by three supporters. Shortly after, she formed the all-women Daughters of Temperance and turned to women's rights.

Susan B. Anthony, a tireless worker for women's suffrage, is the only woman so far to be featured on U.S. currency. The Susan B. Anthony dollar, similar in size and shape to a quarter, was minted from 1979 to 1980.

[32]

Susan B. Anthony met Elizabeth Stanton at a temperance meeting in 1851. They admired each other from the start. This meeting began a friendship that lasted the rest of their lives.

Now the women's movement had the talented leaders to move forward. Elizabeth Stanton provided the genius of ideas in her articles, speeches, and letters to coworkers. Susan Anthony shaped these ideas into a forceful program. Anthony remained unmarried, so she accepted the traveling and organizing duties.

Lucretia Mott served as moral guide. Lucy Stone traveled widely with her new husband, Henry Blackwell, and moved audiences with her speeches. Many other women played important roles. Yet these four launched nationwide activities that changed how people felt about woman suffrage for years to come.

Together the women planned new meetings to trumpet their demands. At first, they relied on the abolition and temperance networks already in place. Then the women organized for their own cause—women's rights. Women in different states traveled to small towns and door to door. They wrote and sold pamphlets for a few pennies to fund their travels. They spoke in churches, in barns, and on railroad platforms—anywhere people gathered.

Stanton found little support for women's right to vote in the early days of the movement. Women showed more interest in seeking property rights, education, or even change in dress. At the time, women wore dresses laced so tightly at the waist with corsets that they could hardly breathe. Layers of heavy skirts and slips dragged on the dusty streets. The corsets and dresses were unhealthy and uncomfortable.

Stanton's cousin Elizabeth Smith Miller showed journalist Amelia Bloomer her new outfit from Europe in 1851. Elizabeth wore baggy pants gathered at the ankle. A skirt shortened to the knee and a loosely belted tunic covered the pants. Bloomer liked the outfit so much she pictured it in her temperance and woman's journal, *The Lily*. Then she sewed a version for herself. The pants were known as bloomers from then on.

Many women wore bloomers for comfort, while some wore them as a sign of protest. Whatever the reason, any woman in pants caused a stir. To those who opposed change for women, bloomers stood for equal rights. Newspapers targeted jokes at bloomer women. Young boys threw mud and yelled insults.

Stanton finally wrote to advise Susan Anthony to wear her old clothes. "It is not wise, Susan," she said, "to use up so much energy and feeling that way [wearing bloomers]."

Before Amelia Bloomer's revolutionary style of dress, women's wardrobes consisted of tight-fitting corsets, heavy skirts, and uncomfortable dresses.

*T*HE FIGHT for the vote and against slavery stayed closely linked until the spring of 1861. For the next four years the vote took a back seat to the Civil War, in which the North and South fought over the issue of slavery. Anthony believed women should continue to press for the vote. Stanton and most women's rights leaders disagreed. Peace was most important now.

After the war, abolitionist leaders were still unwilling to push for woman suffrage. Women were told they must wait their turn. Nothing must upset securing rights for former slaves.

In the summer of 1866, Congress proposed the Fourteenth Amendment to the Constitution. If passed, the amendment would grant citizenship and the right to vote to all "male citizens twenty-one years of age." Then came the Fifteenth Amendment, protecting black men's civil rights. Both amendments excluded women.

Stone, Stanton, and Anthony were stunned. "I will cut off this right arm of mine before I will ever work for or demand the ballot for the Negro and not the woman," Anthony declared. Sojourner Truth, a former slave and noted speaker, called for all women— white and black—to vote.

Francis Harper and other black suffrage leaders felt differently. Harper, a free black from Maryland, was a noted poet and antislavery speaker. "When it was a question of race, she [the black woman] let the lesser question of sex go," she said.

Many women, like Lucy Stone, supported any amendment that meant a better life for blacks. Stanton and Anthony worried that the delay would harm women's chance to vote. The final split between suffrage and antislavery workers came at the 1869 Equal Rights Association convention. Stanton called for an amendment that would grant women the vote. Lucy Stone joined the men in the association and voted against the alarming move.

After the meeting Stanton and Anthony formed the National Woman Suffrage Association (NWSA). The group was open to anyone interested in issues affecting women—particularly the right to vote. They used the weekly suffrage newspaper *The Revolution*, which they had begun in 1868, to air their views.

The following November, Lucy Stone and Henry Blackwell organized the American Woman Suffrage Association (AWSA). Their work centered on achieving state voting rights rather than pushing for an amendment to the federal Constitution. They left issues such as property rights, religion, and divorce to Stanton.

Stone and Blackwell also started the *Woman's Journal* to speak for women professionals. Shortly after, *The Revolution* failed. Still, both groups and their leaders remained active yet bitterly divided for more than twenty years.

Though The Revolution *was a short-lived newspaper, its weekly appearance helped further the suffragist cause.*

6

* *

SMALL STEPS TOWARD SUFFRAGE

The 1871 and 1872 elections brought 150 women in ten states to the polls. They claimed the vote based on their rights as citizens under the Fourteenth Amendment. Some women were never allowed to register. Those who did faced court trials to challenge their vote. With each trial, the women lost.

The most famous woman to test voting laws was Susan B. Anthony. At 7:00 A.M. on November 5, 1872, Anthony, her sisters, and a group of friends marched into a Rochester, New York, barbershop. They expected to be turned away. To everyone's surprise, election registrars allowed the women to sign up and then, several days later, to vote—against federal and state laws.

About two weeks later, a United States marshall appeared at Anthony's door. He arrested Anthony and took her and the fifteen other women who had voted to jail. As ringleader, Anthony was the only woman charged with "illegal voting." Three registrars were accused of taking unlawful ballots from women.

Anthony's upcoming trial captured headlines nationwide. The determined woman used the spotlight to gain support for her case.

[37]

Anthony traveled the country for the next six months to present the woman's side. Her arguments proved so successful that the angry judge moved her trial to another county. The *Rochester Democrat and Chronicle* wrote: ". . .it [the move] is pretty good evidence—unless every man in Monroe County is a fool—that the lady has done no wrong."

The trial was shameful. Judge Hunt denied Anthony the right to speak in court because she was a woman. Then he excused the jury. The judge claimed he had enough proof in Anthony's written ballot. She was guilty. Judge Hunt ordered Anthony to pay a $100 fine. Anthony flatly refused to pay—ever. The judge decided not to jail her. If he did, she could take her case to a higher court.

The three registrars were fined $25. They also refused to pay but were jailed. Suffragists brought the men meals every day. They marched outside the jail, causing an uproar and grabbing newspaper headlines. Parades of women finally shamed the government. President Ulysses S. Grant ordered the men set free.

Anthony and her friends may have lost in court, but their bold moves made more people think about woman suffrage. As a result, breakthroughs for women occurred all throughout the country. Women speaking in public no longer shocked crowds. Many colleges began opening their doors to women. And young women were hanging out signs as doctors and lawyers. One Cleveland woman became a canal boat captain. Women still battled men for equal opportunity and equal pay. But these first steps gave women hope that someday they would vote.

THE FIRST major change in voting laws had begun peacefully three years before. In 1869, Wyoming was a rough-and-tumble new territory. Mainly, it consisted of small cattle and mining towns where men outnumbered women six to one.

One tough Wyoming settler and shopkeeper, Esther Morris, heard Susan B. Anthony talk of women's rights. Soon after, 6-foot (183-centimeter) Morris suggested to community leaders that Wyoming women should vote. She reasoned that women and men built the West together, so why not vote together? Later, Morris's wisdom would gain her a seat as the first woman justice of the peace.

Suffrage supporter and Senate leader William Bright agreed with Morris. He introduced a bill granting women the vote. Before rivals had time to organize, the woman's vote was passed into law.

Alarmed lawmakers feared mobs of women would change the way they ran Wyoming. Women dreaded fights and drunken brawls at saloons where many voted. Worries about the 1870 and 1871 elections proved groundless. Seventy-five-year-old Louisa Swain led the way to the polling booth, the first woman to vote in a major election. Other women followed with husbands or brothers to protect them.

In 1890, Wyoming joined the United States. Washington lawmakers argued that Wyoming should take away women's right to vote. Wyoming leaders insisted they would never trade statehood for women's rights. Wyoming became the first state to include women's right to vote in its constitution since New Jersey, which had let women vote from 1776 to 1807.

Utah was the next territory to follow Wyoming's lead. Utah granted women the vote in 1870, took it away in 1887, and finally restored it in 1896. Each campaign was a terrible struggle.

Susan B. Anthony believed that the state-by-state approach was hopeless. Campaigns relied on small bands of workers in each state. Women had difficulty leaving their home responsibilities.

They had no money of their own to travel. The suffrage movement seriously needed more money and workers.

The temperance movement soon supplied both. Since the Civil War, sale of alcohol had increased. Government received large amounts of money from taxes on alcohol. Therefore, lawmakers overlooked any problems alcohol caused for families.

Homemakers who'd never considered voting gladly entered a war against the evils of alcohol. Respected women picketed saloons and liquor stores. Churchgoers kneeled and prayed on dirty saloon floors until owners closed their doors. Between 1873 and 1874, three thousand saloons closed throughout the country.

Newspapers heralded the successes of the "Woman's War." Local churches supported the women's work. These victories led to the rise of the Women's Christian Temperance Union (WCTU).

The Women's Christian Temperance Union was the largest and most successful women's organization of its time.

Under Frances Willard, an educated and appealing suffrage worker, the WCTU became the largest women's group in the nation. Money and volunteers flowed into the WCTU to end alcohol sales. Willard, a friend of Anthony's, cleverly expanded the group's aims to include voting rights. Her "Home Protection" program required that women be allowed to vote so they could protect families against "liquor and other vices."

As the WCTU expanded, so did protests from wealthy alcohol interests. Then the bond between temperance and suffrage became a major problem. Brewers, saloonkeepers, and liquor salesmen pressured lawmakers to oppose any laws giving women more rights. Susan B. Anthony tried to distance suffrage from the temperance movement. Still, many tough state campaigns were lost to liquor money. For decades, men believed the woman's vote was merely a way to end alcohol sales.

By the late 1800s suffrage groups had gained a great deal of acceptance in Congress and at the state level. Anthony and Stanton fought any battle that produced more rights for women. They held conventions in Washington, D.C., hoping to sway lawmakers. Senator A. A. Sargent introduced the "Anthony Amendment" into Congress in 1878, beginning the uphill battle for support. Lucy Stone and her husband kept to their state-by-state approach, forming a well-organized network through local groups. Many women's voices spoke through their *Woman's Journal*.

Over the years the leaders' differences lessened. The pioneers of women's rights were growing old. Lucretia Mott had died in 1880. Alice Stone Blackwell, Lucy's daughter, handled much of her parents' business. Susan B. Anthony traveled with a devoted younger assistant, Anna Shaw. The time was right to merge the two groups and train new, younger leaders.

In 1890, the two rival women's rights groups combined into the National American Woman Suffrage Association (NAWSA). Stanton became the first president. She led the National American until 1892; the next year Lucy Stone died. Anthony followed Stanton as president for another eight years. She remained a popular and active leader until age eighty-six.

In 1906, Anthony gave her last public address at the NAWSA convention in Baltimore, Maryland. Although she was weak, her spirit never faded. "The fight must not cease: you must see that it does not stop," she proclaimed. One month later Anthony died, leaving a new generation of women to press for women's rights.

7

FROM JAIL TO VICTORY

During the early 1900s the National American made little progress. Without its colorful pioneers, life left the movement. Then another group of women—factory workers—entered the suffrage battle.

With more women working, women outnumbered men in some industries, especially clothing. These women withstood twelve- and fourteen-hour workdays six or seven days a week. They faced unsafe, dirty, and noisy workplaces for low wages. Many factory women believed the vote would give them the power to improve these conditions.

Melinda Scott, a New York hat trimmer, argued, "I do not want to be governor of the State . . . but I do want the ballot to be able to register my protest against the conditions that are killing and maiming."

Factory workers changed the way women battled unfair treatment. They took their fight to the streets in larger numbers. In 1909 and 1910 women workers organized major strikes against textile and clothing manufacturers in New York City, Philadelphia, and Chicago. Women dared to leave jobs and form picket lines until their demands were met. "We Strike for Justice," read their banners.

Suffrage women who longed for action took notice. In New York City, some joined striking marchers on picket lines. Wealthy supporters collected money to free women arrested by the police. Others appealed to judges for fairer treatment of arrested strikers. Gradually, the woman suffrage movement became linked to the cry for better working conditions.

In 1910 the two groups arranged the first suffrage parade in New York City. Hundreds of National American members wearing yellow "Votes for Women" sashes walked up Fifth Avenue beside their sister workers. Others rode in decorated cars proudly waving banners and flags. The colorful parade attracted hordes of busy shoppers and became an ever-larger yearly event. By the third year, *The New York Times* reported "20,000 marchers and 500,000 onlookers."

During this time, state organizations made some inroads. The first breakthroughs since the success in Utah fourteen years before came in the West. The state of Washington passed the woman's vote in 1910. The following year California women triumphed, but only after a fierce battle.

After California's success, big-business owners joined liquor interests to oppose women in other states. Businessmen claimed that suffrage women supported social programs for workers. If women gained the vote, companies feared they would lose money to fairer wages and safer factories for workers.

Businessmen backed anyone who opposed the loosely run National American in each state. They bought votes from immigrants,

In this New York City suffrage march, women carry the boxes, called rostrums, on which they stood to give speeches urging women's rights.

many of whom couldn't speak English, and stuffed ballot boxes. When that failed, they paid election judges to report incorrect vote counts.

By 1912, energy for state suffrage campaigns reached a new low. The woman's vote passed in Arizona, Oregon, and Kansas but lost in Michigan, Ohio, and Wisconsin. Southern states still refused to consider woman suffrage. Instead, they enacted voting taxes to keep poor black men from voting. Southern white men resisted sharing power and government with anyone.

*A*LICE PAUL was just the person to breathe life into the dying movement. Paul was a Quaker and social worker who traveled to England for more schooling. In England, she discovered that women struggled for the vote, too. But they threw notes wrapped around rocks, picketed, and held hunger strikes—anything to attract the attention of lawmakers.

When Paul returned to the United States, she found only six suffrage states, with four million voting women. She wanted this voting power focused on the president and congressmen, who could change the federal Constitution. Paul asked to chair the National American congressional committee to try her plan.

Paul worked tirelessly at her own expense. She would not take "no" for an answer. In record time, she opened a Washington office, raised money, and organized a core of dedicated workers. Within two months, she arranged the committee's first protest.

On March 3, 1913, President Woodrow Wilson arrived in Washington for his inauguration. He was surprised to find only a small turnout to greet him at the train station. Instead, the crowds were on Pennsylvania Avenue, watching five thousand suffragists march. The march resulted in near riots. Howling mobs of men lined the streets. Enraged onlookers insulted marchers. Many tripped or grabbed the women. Police stood guard but provided little protection. The women were treated so badly that Congress appointed a special committee to investigate.

Julia Lathrop told the committee:

There was quite a file of young men . . . making the most insulting remarks to the women. They tore a woman's suffrage badge from off my coat and nearly knocked me down. . . . A woman cried out . . . that they had torn two children away from her.

[46]

The March 1913 suffragette parade in Washington, D.C., which attracted more attention than the arrival of the new president, Woodrow Wilson.

The nation was outraged. Paul took advantage of the attention by circulating petitions and staging marches in Washington. She met with President Wilson to urge his support of a bill granting women the vote.

In June, the state of Illinois granted women the right to vote in presidential elections, becoming the first state east of the Mississippi River to champion at least partial woman suffrage. The next month 531 people from different states presented a petition with 200,000 signatures to the United States Senate.

The president and Congress seemed unmoved. Both said women should appeal to individual states for the vote. Paul had a better idea. Why not work to vote Democrats, President Wilson's political party, out of office in the 1914 election? Democrats were the party in power who refused to grant women the vote.

Carrie Chapman Catt and other National American leaders disagreed with Paul's approach. Catt, who served as National American's president from 1900 to 1904, was a masterful fundraiser and planner who reorganized the association after Anthony died. In 1913, she reappeared as the group's leader, bringing new energy to the National American. Catt rejected any work for one political party over another. Instead, she introduced her secret "Winning Plan," combining a state-by-state drive with polite appeals to President Wilson for a federal amendment.

Paul grew impatient with Catt's behind-the-scenes plan. She split from the National American and formed what would become the National Woman's Party, which began more startling activities. Party women swarmed state and county fairs, mining camps, and hospital balls. They held mass meetings and traveled door-to-door, even to small farms. Giant purple, white, and gold Woman's Party banners hung across town streets and arched over parades.

The Democrats won most state and national elections in 1914. But the National Woman's Party made women a serious threat to anyone running for office. After the election, Democratic party chairman Vance McCormick admitted: "We must get rid of the Suffrage Amendment before 1918 if we want to control the next Congress."

Paul continued the battle in Washington. The National Woman's Party flooded the president and Congress with letters, telegrams, petitions, mass meetings, and car caravans from across the nation. The first suffrage debate in the House of Representatives occurred on January 12, 1915. Although suffrage lost, women were hopeful. On December 4, 1916, National Woman's Party members filled the gallery in the House to hear President Wilson's address to Congress. At a signal, five women dropped a huge yellow satin banner over the balcony. It read, "Mr. President, what will you do for woman suffrage?"

On January 10, 1917, the Woman's Party arranged around-the-clock pickets at the White House. Paul wanted to remind President Wilson that women held him responsible for their not voting. The women held banners, waved flags, and passed out papers. They camped outside the White House for three months without a problem.

Then the United States entered World War I. Protesters attacked the women, claiming they were disloyal to the country. Still, the pickets continued. They burned copies of the president's speeches and lit Watchfires of Freedom. Women wanted the same equal rights at home that the country was fighting for overseas.

Police began arresting picketers for blocking traffic. Other women quickly replaced them. Over the next six months more than two hundred women faced trials. Alice Paul and ninety-six others who refused to pay their fines were thrown into filthy jails and workhouses for up to six months. Guards beat and isolated troublemakers in cells. When women refused to eat, they were force-fed. Lucy Burns wrote:

[We] were dragged through halls by force, our clothing partly removed by force, and we were examined. . . . Dr. Gannon told me then I must be fed. I was held down by five people at legs, arms and head. Gannon pushed tube up left nostril. . . . It hurts nose and throat very much. . . . Food dumped directly into stomach feels like a ball of lead.

[49]

Reports of cruel treatment outraged the nation. On November 28, President Wilson ordered the women set free. The White House pickets remained. Members of the National American, with Catt as their president since 1915, disliked Paul's tactics and kept their distance. Still, the party's daring moves opened many doors that strengthened Catt's state groups. Paul's antics forced the president and Congress to take action.

Meanwhile, the climate in the country had changed. Since 1900, a reform movement called progressivism had swept over the nation. Citizens wanted their rights to be better protected. They wanted more laws to curb big business. And more people were joining the temperance movement. Suffragists began to seem much less radical during this period, known as the Progressive Era. By the outbreak of World War I in 1914, the question was no longer *if* women would vote, but *when*.

Women played a major role in World War I. Overseas, they served as nurses and in desk jobs to free men for battle. At home, women filled jobs in weapons factories and other industries after men left for war. President Wilson finally agreed that women who worked as men should vote as men. He asked legislators to reconsider the Nineteenth, or "Anthony," Amendment, which had first been introduced in 1878. He told senators on September 30, 1918: "We have made partners of the women in this war; shall we admit them only to a partnership of suffering and . . . not to a partnership of privilege and right?"

The Anthony Amendment lost by only two votes. On May 19, 1919, President Wilson called a special session of the House of Representatives to vote again on the amendment. After two days of debate, 304 representatives voted for suffrage. By then, suffrage senators knew they had enough votes. On June 4, 1919, the Senate passed the Nineteenth Amendment to the Constitution.

Although the suffragist movement sparked some controversial episodes, most male crowds were respectful, attentive, and supportive of the women who spoke.

THE AMENDMENT needed the approval of thirty-six states to become law. Now the fight switched to the states. Catt rallied her state teams. Women coaxed governors into calling special sessions for lawmakers to vote on the amendment. By June 16, Illinois, Wisconsin, Michigan, Pennsylvania, Massachusetts, and Ohio had approved, or ratified, the amendment.

During the summer few states called for a vote. Women eager to vote offered to raise money for a special session in Oregon. They began petition drives in Indiana and throughout the West. Even with strong opposition from liquor and big-business interests, thirty-five states ratified the amendment by March 22, 1920.

Only three remaining states seemed likely to approve the amendment. Of these, in Vermont and Connecticut governors flatly refused to call a special session. The only hope was Tennessee.

Forces opposed to women's right to vote rushed to Nashville. For two months they fought one of the most bitter suffrage battles in decades. Nevertheless, on August 18, 1920, Tennessee became the thirty-sixth state to approve woman suffrage. Eight days later the Nineteenth Amendment to the Constitution was signed into law—in time for some 26 million women to vote in the November 1920 election.

AFTERWORD

THE DREAM CONTINUES

The major changes that men feared would result from women voting never happened. Businesses still thrived. A "women's voting bloc" never swept lawmakers from office. Women did not group together behind issues. They voted individually—as men did—to reflect their beliefs.

Political parties initially welcomed women. But the women soon found themselves assigned to separate "women's divisions" or office work. Wyoming's Jeanette Rankin took office as the first congresswoman in 1917, and Oklahoma's Alice Robertson joined her in 1921. Otherwise, women usually stayed out of office. Politics and government continued much the same.

After suffrage, Carrie Chapman Catt devoted herself to a new group, the League of Women Voters. The League replaced the National American and focused on teaching women how to be good citizens. Today, the League informs voters about elections. Its state branches fight for fairer laws and better government.

Unlike Catt, Alice Paul urged her National Woman's Party to continue much as before. Now the group opposed any laws that assumed women deserved fewer rights than men. Paul decided the best way to make certain of fair treatment was through an equal rights amendment. At the seventy-fifth anniversary of the first Seneca Falls Convention, Paul presented her Lucretia Mott Amendment. A new woman's movement for equal rights was born.

Women made little progress for the next few decades. World War II sent men away as soldiers. Again, women took jobs usually held by men. Once the war ended, however, most returned to homemaking.

Another major push for black civil rights came during the 1960s. Black and white women joined protest groups, just as they had taken on the abolitionist cause before the Civil War. But once again women were kept from running these groups. In the 1960s women were quick to realize that they had "unfinished business" from suffrage days.

Betty Friedan, a journalist and discontented homemaker, wrote about women's place in *The Feminine Mystique*. She believed that television and magazines misled people with a false picture of women as happy homemakers. Her book became a best-seller. It also awakened many women's desire to have more choices in their lives.

In 1966, Friedan founded the National Organization for Women (NOW) to "bring women into the mainstream of America, now, . . . in fully equal partnership with men." Within one year NOW had 1,200 members. As the group grew, it championed women's right to equal treatment at home and the workplace. Today, NOW is the country's largest women's rights group. One of its major goals is to pass the Equal Rights Amendment written by Alice Paul.

Many new doors opened because of suffrage and the women's movement. Women entered careers previously closed to them. They orbited the Earth as astronauts and saved lives as firefighters. Opportunities expanded in government as well. In 1969, Shirley Chisholm broke new ground when she was sworn in as the first black congresswoman. Another major breakthrough was Sandra Day O'Connor's appointment to the U.S. Supreme Court in 1980, the first time a woman was named to the Court in its 191-year history. Geraldine Ferraro surprised voters in the 1984 election as the first woman to run for vice president on a leading party ticket.

By 1992 the number of women in elected offices rose to 22 percent. So many women gained seats as governors, congresswomen, and local representatives that reporters named 1992 "The Year of the Woman." Yet rising numbers told only part of the story.

Yes, women held important posts in government. But they earned 35 percent less than men in similar government jobs, and the trend extended into most workplaces. In many cases, men continue to hold better jobs and earn more money. Because they run government and most companies, men make key decisions that affect women's lives.

Every August 26 is National Women's Equality Day. The day honors those women who gave countless years of their lives and millions of dollars for the freedom to vote. The day also serves as a reminder of all women have accomplished since Seneca Falls and all that remains to be done. Without the power of the vote, however, women could never even dream of equal rights.

Equal Rights Amendment

ALICE PAUL wrote the Equal Rights Amendment (ERA) in 1923. Each following year Congress voted on the amendment and failed to pass it. Then the House approved these words in 1971: "Equality of rights under the law shall not be denied or abridged by the United States or any State on account of sex."

The Senate voted for the amendment in 1972. Women's groups around the country launched major rallies and petition drives. Within a year, thirty states had approved the amendment. Eight more states were needed to ratify it, but they never did, even after Congress extended the deadline to June 30, 1982. The amendment was lost, at least for the time being. Too many state legislators feared that if women were granted equal rights, they would refuse to play their central role in raising children and in homemaking. Some ideas die slowly.

Chronology

1840   Lucretia Mott and Elizabeth Cady Stanton meet at the World Anti-Slavery Convention in London.

1848   The first Woman's Rights Convention is held in Seneca Falls, New York, where, for the first time in the United States, women demand the vote.

1850   The first National Women's Rights Convention meets in Worcester, Massachusetts. Lucy Stone joins the suffrage movement.

1851   Susan B. Anthony meets Elizabeth Cady Stanton. Amelia Bloomer popularizes "bloomers."

1869   Susan B. Anthony and Elizabeth Cady Stanton form the National Woman Suffrage Association to gain voting rights for women through constitutional amendment.

        Lucy Stone and Henry Blackwell organize the American Woman Suffrage Association for state approval of woman suffrage.

        Wyoming becomes the first territory to allow women to vote in all elections.

1872   Susan B. Anthony votes, is arrested, and receives an unfair trial in which the judge finds her guilty.

1874   Women's Christian Temperance Union (WCTU) is formed.

1878   California Senator A. A. Sargent introduces the Anthony Amendment into Congress for the first time.

1890   The National Woman Suffrage Association and American Woman Suffrage Association merge into the National American Woman Suffrage Association (NAWSA).

1910   Washington state becomes the first state in fourteen years to grant women the vote.

1912   Alice Paul chairs the National American congressional committee in Washington, D.C.

1915   Alice Paul forms the National Woman's Party. Carrie Chapman Catt becomes president of NAWSA.

1916   Carrie Chapman Catt puts her "Winning Plan" into action to gain woman suffrage through state organizations and presidential appeals.

1917   National Woman's Party women picket the White House for ten months, resulting in two hundred arrests and much public attention.

1919   On May 19 President Woodrow Wilson calls a special session of the House of Representatives to consider a constitutional amendment granting women the vote. Two days later it passes. On June 4, the Senate votes in favor of the suffrage amendment.

1920   On August 18, Tennessee becomes the thirty-sixth state to vote for the Nineteenth Amendment, thereby making it law.

Further Reading

Blumberg, Rhoda. *Bloomers!* New York: Bradbury Press, 1993.

Coolidge, Olivia. *Women's Rights: The Suffrage Movement in America, 1848– 1920*. New York: E. P. Dutton, 1966.

Corbin, Carole Lynn. *Issues in American History: The Right to Vote*. New York: Franklin Watts, 1985.

Faber, Doris. *Petticoat Politics*. New York: Lothrop, Lee & Shepard, 1967.

Oneal, Zibby. *A Long Way to Go*. New York: Viking, 1990. (This is a work of fiction.)

Severn, Bill. *The Right to Vote*. New York: Ives Washburn, 1972.

Smith, Betsy Covington. *Women Win the Vote*. Englewood Cliffs, NJ: Silver Burdett Press, 1989.

Stein, R. Conrad. *The Story of the Nineteenth Amendment*. Chicago: Childrens Press, 1982.

Sullivan, George. *The Day the Women Got the Vote: A Photo History of the Women's Rights Movement*. New York: Scholastic, 1994.

Bibliography

A special thanks to the bright and thoughtful women suffragists who wrote histories, biographies, and diaries. They documented their struggles to remind future generations about a time when the woman's vote was merely a dream.

Cooney, Robert. "Taking a New Look—The Enduring Significance of the American Woman Suffrage Movement." "And Still They Persevered . . . A Brief History." *Women Win the Vote*. Windsor, CA: National Women's History Project, 1994.

DuBois, Ellen Carol, ed. *Elizabeth Cady Stanton, Susan B. Anthony, Correspondence, Writings, Speeches*. New York: Schocken Books, 1981.

DuBois, Ellen Carol. *Feminism and Suffrage: The Emergence of an Independent Women's Movement in America 1848–1869*. Ithaca, NY: Cornell University Press, 1978.

Flexnor, Eleanor. *Century of Struggle: The Women's Rights Movement in the United States*. Cambridge, MA: The Belknap Press, 1976.

Frost, Elizabeth, and Kathryn Cullen-DuPont. *Women's Suffrage in America*. New York: Facts on File, 1992.

Irwin, Inez Haynes. *The Story of Alice Paul and The National Woman's Party.* Fairfax, VA: Denlinger's Publishers, 1977.

Kilgore, Kathleen. "The Suffragette's Dress." *Yankee,* May 1991, p. 144.

Kraditor, Aileen. *The Ideas of the Woman Suffrage Movement, 1890–1920.* New York: Columbia University Press, 1965.

Livermore, Mary, Lucy Stone, Julia Ward Howe, and William Lloyd Garrison, eds. "Woman Suffrage Meetings," March 10, 1870. "The Woman's Rights Movement," January 8, 1870. "What Is the Remedy?" January 22, 1870. *The Woman's Journal.*

Myron, Nancy, and Charlotte Bunch, eds. *Women Remembered.* Baltimore: Diana Press, 1974.

Peck, Mary Gray. *Carrie Chapman Catt: A Biography.* New York: H. W. Wilson, 1944.

Perry, Elizabeth. "Why Suffrage for American Women Was Not Enough." *History Today,* September 1993, pp. 36–42.

Porter, Kirk. *A History of Suffrage in the United States.* New York: Greenwood Press, 1918.

Read, Phyllis, and Bernard Witlieb. *The Book of Women's Firsts.* New York: Random House, 1992.

Reynolds, Moira Davison. *Women Champions of Human Rights.* Jefferson, NC: McFarland & Company, 1991.

Stanton, Elizabeth Cady. *The History of Woman Suffrage,* Vol. I–VI, ed. Susan B. Anthony and Ida Husted Harper. National American Woman Suffrage Association. North Stratford, NH: The Arno Press, 1969.

Stanton, Theodore, and Harriot Stanton Blatch, eds. *Elizabeth Cady Stanton.* New York: Arno & The New York Times, 1969.

Van Voris, Jacqueline. *Carrie Chapman Catt: A Public Life.* New York: The Feminist Press, 1987.

Wheeler, Leslie, ed. *Loving Warriors: Selected Letters of Lucy Stone and Henry B. Blackwell,* 1853–1893. New York: The Dial Press, 1981.

Index